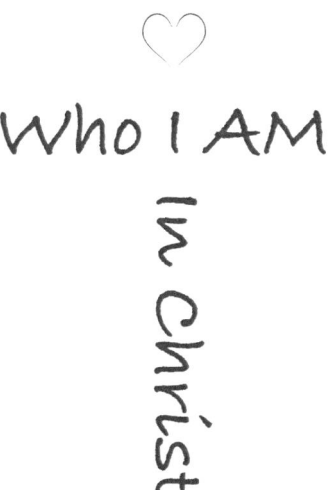

Who I AM in Christ

Written & Illustrated by Darcy Jackson

Published by Fictitious Ink Publishing, Tumbler Ridge,
BC, Canada, V0C 2W0

This booklet is devoted to
Lord Jesus Christ
and dedicated to
my friend and sister in Christ,
Tracy.
Thanks for your encouragement
and exceptional work.
I love you,
Darcy

I AM
Alive in Christ
because the Spirit of the
Great I AM
lives in me.

I am
I am
I am a child of God
I AM
saved by grace
redeemed by Jesus
loved & forgiven

3

Ephesians 1 : 5
In love, God predestined
us to be ADOPTED

as His children
through Jesus Christ

I AM adopted into the family of God

Thank You Jesus

1 John 5 : 1
Everyone who believes that Jesus is the Christ is BORN of God

1 Peter 1 : 23
For you have been BORN AGAIN,...
through the living and enduring Word of God.

I AM born again

Thank You Jesus

1 John 3 : 1
How great is the love that
the Father has lavished on us
that we should be called
CHILDREN of God!

And that is what we are!

I AM a child of God
Thank You Jesus

Psalm 34 : 4
I sought the Lord, and
He answered me;

He DELIVERED me
from all my fears.

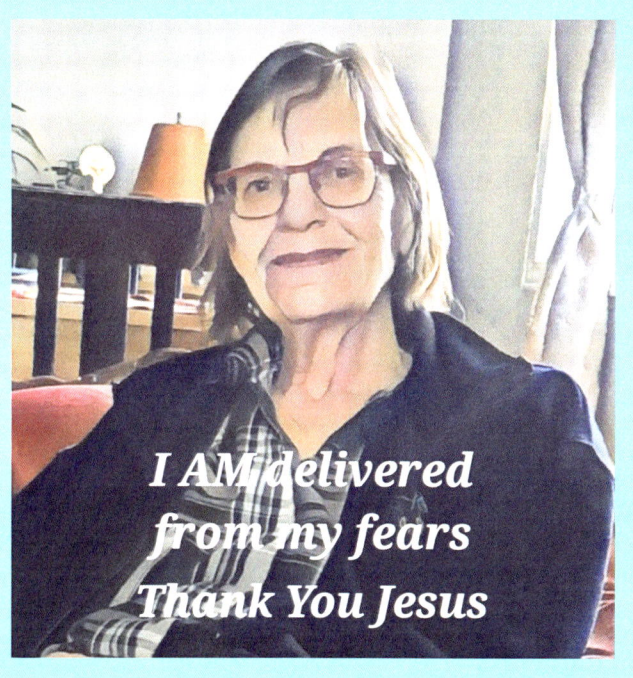

I AM delivered
from my fears
Thank You Jesus

Hebrews 13 : 20, 21
May the God of peace,...
EQUIP you with everything
good for doing His will,

E

and may He work in us
what is pleasing to Him,
through Jesus Christ

Acts 10 : 43
All the prophets testify
about Jesus Christ; that
everyone who believes in Him

F

receives FORGIVENESS
of sins through
His Name.

I AM forgiven
Thank You Jesus

Romans 11 : 19, 20
You will say then,
"Branches were broken off
so that I could be
GRAFTED in".

Granted. But they were
broken off because of unbelief
and you stand by faith.

17

1 Peter 2 : 24
Christ Himself bore our sins
in His body on the tree, so that
we might die to sins and
live for righteousness;

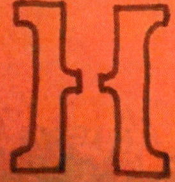

by His wounds
you have been
HEALED.

2 Corinthians 5 : 17
Therefore, if anyone is
IN CHRIST,
they are a new creation:

the old has gone,
the new has come!

I AM in Christ
Tha... Jesu...

Romans 3 : 23, 24
For all have sinned and
fall short of the glory of
God,

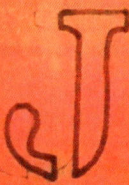

and are JUSTIFIED freely
by His grace through the
redemption that came by
Jesus Christ.

I AM justified freely by grace

MESSIAH

Thank You Jesus

John 10 : 14
"I AM the Good Shepherd:
I KNOW My sheep and
My sheep KNOW Me".

John 10 : 27
My sheep listen to My voice;
I KNOW them, and
they follow Me.

I AM known by the Good Shepherd Thank You Jesus

Ephesians 3 : 17, 18, 19
And I pray that you, being
rooted and established in
LOVE, may have power,
together with all the saints,

L

to grasp how wide and long
and high and deep is the
LOVE of Christ, and to know
this LOVE that surpasses
knowledge

I AM loved very deeply
Thank You Jesus

Genesis 5 : 1, 2
When God created man,
He MADE him in the
likeness of God.

**He created them
male and female.**

I AM made in the image of God Thank You Jesus

Ephesians 4 : 22, 23, 24
You were taught,...
to be made NEW in the
attitude of your minds; and
to put on the NEW self,

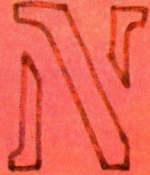

created to be like God
in true righteousness
and holiness.

Thank You Jesus

I AM new in You

1 John 5 : 4
Everyone born of God
OVERCOMES the world.

This is the victory that has
OVERCOME the world,
even our faith.

Romans 5 : 1
Therefore, since we have
been justified through faith,
we have PEACE with God

P

through our
Lord Jesus Christ.

Zephaniah 3 : 17
The Lord your God is with you.
He is mighty to save. He will take
great delight in you. He will
QUIET you with His love.

He will rejoice over you
with singing.

I AM quiet in Your love

Thank You Jesus

Colossians 1 : 21, 22
Once you were alienated
from God,... But now He has
RECONCILED you
by Christ's physical body

R

through death, to present you holy
in His sight, without blemish and
free from accusation.

I AM reconciled
to God

Thank You Jesus

Ephesians 2 : 4, 5
Because of His great love
for us, God, who is rich in
mercy, made us alive with
Christ

even when we were dead
in transgressions -
it is by grace you have
been SAVED.

I AM saved by grace
Thank You Jesus

Philippians 3 : 20, 21
Our citizenship is in heaven.
And we eagerly await a Savior
from there, the Lord Jesus Christ,
who, by the power that

enables Him to bring
everything under His control,
will TRANSFORM our lowly
bodies so that they will be like
His glorious body.

1 John 2 : 28
And now, dear children,
continue in Him, so that
when He appears,

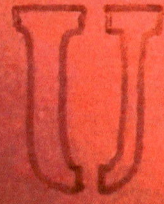

we may be confident and
UNASHAMED
before Him at His coming.

1 Corinthians 15 : 56, 57
The sting of death is sin,
and the power of sin is the
law.

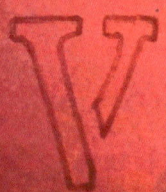

But thanks be to God!
He gives us the VICTORY
through our Lord Jesus
Christ.

Ephesians 2 : 8, 9, 10
For it is by grace you have been
saved, through faith -
and this is not from yourselves,
it is the gift of God -

not by works, so that no one
can boast. For we are God's
WORKMANSHIP, created in
Christ Jesus to do good works

I AM the workmanship
of God in Christ
Thank You Jesus

1 Corinthians 11 : 1
Follow my EXAMPLE,
as I follow the EXAMPLE
of Christ.

Philippians 3 : 17
Join with others in
following
my EXAMPLE

I AM an example of a follower in Christ. Thank You Jesus.

Matthew 11 : 28, 29, 30
"Come to Me, all you who
are weary and burdened,
and I will give you rest.
Take My YOKE upon you

and learn from Me, for
I AM gentle and humble in
heart, and you will find rest
for your souls. For My YOKE
is easy; my burden is light."

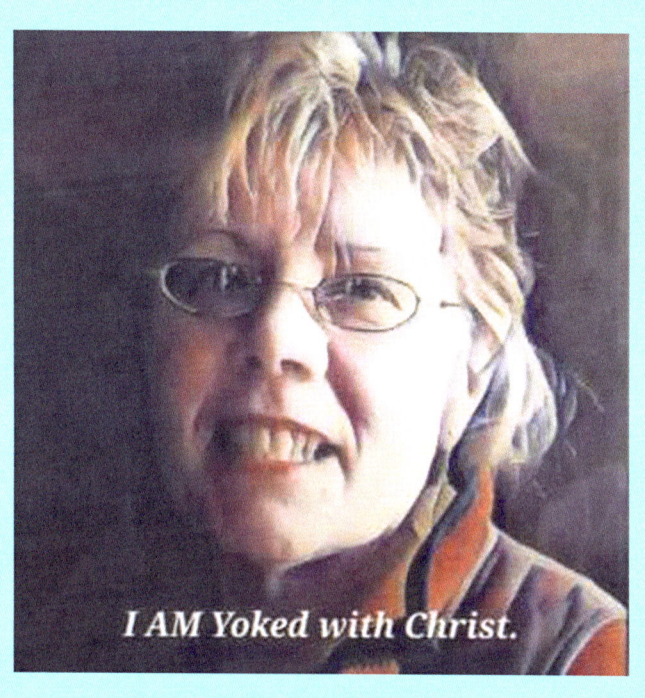

I AM Yoked with Christ.

53

Galatians 4 : 18
It is fine to be ZEALOUS,
provided the purpose
is good

and to be so always
and not just when
I am with you.

I AM zealous for good
Thank You Jesus

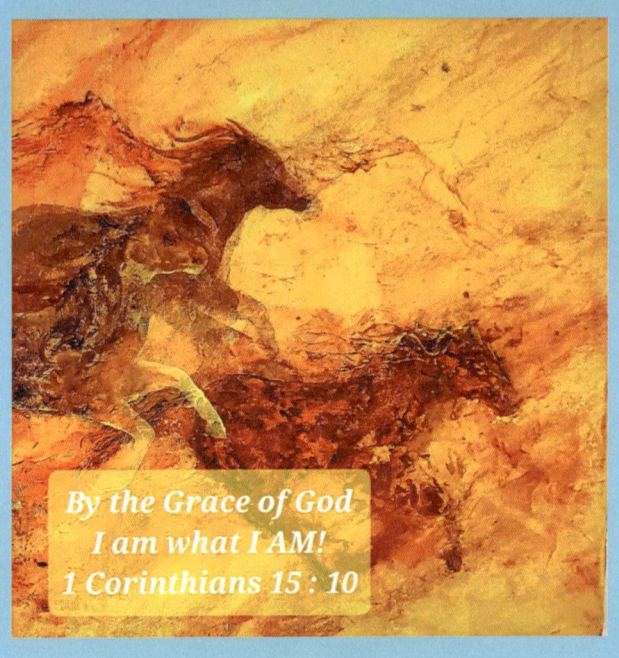

By the Grace of God
I am what I AM!
1 Corinthians 15 : 10

Thank You Father
for sending Your Son
into our world
to save us and redeem us.
Thank You Lord
that I AM yours
and You are mine.
I AM forever grateful.

More in the series!

We hope you found this inspirational
pocketbook uplifting. The simple
affirmative statements, illustrations,
and scriptures were prayerfully compiled
by the author to bring you
strength and peace.

Plus, there are more books in the series!
They'd make a beautiful gift for someone
you love. Available at select bookstores
and online. God bless!

*If you enjoyed this book, please consider
leaving a positive rating or review.*

www.ingramcontent.com/pod-product-compliance
Lightning Source LLC
Chambersburg PA
CBRC090835120626
46547CB00011B/699

TOASTS
AND FORMS
OF PUBLIC
ADDRESS

for Those Who Wish to Say the
Right Thing in the Right Way

William Pittenger

Modern Vaudeville Press

Toasts and Forms of Public Address:

for Those Who Wish to Say the Right Thing in
the Right Way

By William Pittenger
Foreword by Thom Wall

Layout © 2023 by Modern Vaudeville Press

Modern Vaudeville Press
113 E. Mayland St.
Philadelphia, PA 19144
USA
www.modernvaudevillepress.com
info@modernvaudevillepress.com

ISBN: 978-1-958604-07-6
Library of Congress: 2023920735